ways to wander

edited by

Clare Qualmann & Claire Hind

Published in this first edition in 2015 by:
Triarchy Press
Axminster EX13 5PF, England

+44 (0)1297 631456
info@triarchypress.net
www.triarchypress.net

Paperback ISBN: 978-1-909470-72-9
ePub ISBN: 978-1-909470-73-6
pdf ISBN: 978-1-909470-74-3

This book is an output of the AHRC funded 'Footwork' project, part of the Walking Artists Network, with additional support from the Centre for Performing Arts Development at the University of East London.
www.walkingartistsnetwork.org
www.footworkwalk.wordpress.com
www.uel.ac.uk/cpad

Front cover photo by Claire Hind, taken during a Footwork research group walk toward Lelant, St Ives Bay, 2015

Ink drawings (before 'Ways' 9, 29 and 45) by Clare Qualmann

Other 'Ways' illustrated by their authors

Dear wanderer,

The many and varied ways to wander detailed herein range from the geographically specific to the generally located. Where these specificities exclude you please feel free to adapt or reimagine to suit. We advise that you prepare for your wander so please note that they sit somewhere on a scale between dream and reality, certain routes may have changed and others may be close to the edge.

So, take care and consider your safety and the safety of others before venturing out. Enjoy.

Clare and Claire

1. River Rural; River Urban

An Urban/Rural psychogeographic exploration.

To be done either in one day or over a period of several days or as an ongoing research project.

Choose a river in a city or a town.

Decide where the most significant point of the river is in the urban area.

Find out where the river's source is.

Go to the source. Take a photograph or make a drawing of the source. Write notes about the source. Note any ambiguities as to what is the actual source.

Walk from the source to the point on the river in the town or city you have chosen. (This can be done in one go or in sections). Take photographs, make drawings, take notes as you go. Note how you have to take diversions around private land.

Reflect on the fact that there are parts of the river you will never see.

When you arrive at your town or city river point take a photograph, make a drawing and take notes.

Reflect on the fact that the water has come from the source to this point and flows on.

Note how the journey of the river changed as you walked along it.

Note how your journey changed as you walked along it.

Compare the source with the end point.

Now walk the route in reverse.

Repeat, doing the same from town/city river to mouth of river.

2. Feeling and Touching: a tactile-kinaesthetic walk

> A very simple way in is to start by feeling the ground beneath your feet. Notice how you shift your centre of gravity, what your body does to keep your balance or soften the impact of each step in response to different surfaces – concrete, paving, turf, mud, ice, sand… You don't have to change how you walk, just take an interest in what's going on.>>

>> Then you can experiment – look out for different surfaces to walk on, try different speeds or spread your weight between a soft and a hard surface or a slippery and a bumpy one. Avoid nothing; take an interest in everything: even dogshit can be interesting to walk on if you have an experimental approach.>>>

>>> Another simple activity: touch the surfaces you see. Use your hand or face or the skin elsewhere on your body (easier in summer) to sample texture, hardness and temperature. You could touch everything (which will definitely slow down your walk) or sample surfaces from time to time. On an everyday urban walk I can find different sorts of brick, bark, metal, moss, stone, leaves, concrete, earth, sand, blossom, wood, glass, fabric, standing water, running water, cat, dog, rubber, plastic… How long can your skin hold the memory of what you've just touched?>>>>

>>>> Or: try imagining the feel of everything you see, and check the accuracy of your sensory imagination from time to time by touching something. If there's a mismatch, does that matter? With practice, perhaps your brain will start directly converting the visual to the tactile and you can feel the landscape on your skin without thinking.><lll

From: Claire Hind (C.Hind)
Sent: 21 May 2014 07:26
To: Clare Qualmann (c.qualmann)
Subject: Ways to Wander project

Dear Clare,

Walking is both a controlled, limited and rule-based activity and a free, spontaneous and improvised experience. Rebecca Solnit's *Wanderlust* calls upon the seriousness of walking and also its playfulness.

My childhood consisted of repetitive acts of hiking in the mountains of Wales and always with a task of getting around a lake, or scrambling to the top of a rock - but never a summit, as a family of 6 we could never quite make it that far — because the clouds came down and the weather changed pretty rapidly, I recall. Still, we set off every week even in the worst of weathers and we hiked with purpose but with jokes and laughter, sometimes tears. I remember once being scared of some boggy terrain convinced it was sinking sand and I prayed that the soggy landscape underneath my feet wouldn't feed me to the mud troll. At the age of 7, the site of Tryfan, always dark, perpetually in shadow towering above me, tall and fierce was both exciting and terrifying like a sleeping dinosaur that could wake at any moment.

Solnit's walking that wanders so readily into religion, philosophy, landscape, urban policy, anatomy, allegory and heartbreak shaped my past and paved my future, if there is ever a pilgrimage then it is the walk that slips between Ludus (serious play) and Paidia (free play) — which Roger Caillois talks about in his book *Man, Play and Games*.

Claire

For years, I have used the metaphor of wandering to help explain how I understand the central creative process I believe to be at the heart of design. In using the word design, I wish to include artists, musicians and architects: the word design refers to a shared creative process.

Imagine the following. You go into the countryside and start walking. You maybe have a small hamper with you, or some food in a rucksack. You walk along a bit, and after a time see something you think you might walk towards. In a while, you change your mind and walk off the path through some trees, with no idea where you're going. Well, you've had no idea where you are going all along: you are wandering. You find a path, follow it, come to a junction and decide to go one way or the other. After a bit you decide to go and take the other branch. Perhaps you can still see that something, but probably not.

So it goes on.

After a bit you come to a place that you just like. Perhaps the sun is out. You are quietly by yourself. It's peaceful, birds sing, the grass is inviting.

Somehow, without any particular criteria, perhaps without even realising it, you feel this is the place to stop. You sit down, get out your picnic, eat and drink. This is wonderful. You realise that your wandering has acquired a purpose: to arrive at this place. You can look back at your wandering journey and pretend it was logical and sensible and ordered! You did not know it before and you could not have described it, But it's right. Everything fits in place. The walk takes form as leading you here.

If that sounds to you like a metaphor for design, I am glad.

4. Crossing Paths/Different Worlds in Abney Park Cemetery

Upon entering the Victorian gates on Stoke Newington High Street, ignore (or not) the Strong Brew-favouring vagabonds who have made the right-hand corner their local. Walk with me towards the overhanging gloom, tread the worn path that takes you to the left. There is such a clash of histories in this anachronistic space. Crooked stones being swallowed up by lush and greedy nature, beaten back kindly by the Friends of Abney Park Cemetery — their eternal merry war. Let's leave the jogging traffic and laughter of this open space to take a turn to the right into this first side path. The branches overhead and vines ever climbing create a little silence for you and me. What shoes are you wearing? Feel like a scramble? You're not supposed to (shhhh) but here up on the left we can climb (respectfully) through the gravestones to an even more secluded spot. Here.

This is where my best thinking gets done. Amidst these voices long-silenced I find my voice. A little secret place of quiet away from the main path where other trajectories are being lived. It's a funny thing, crossing paths, different worlds. There is no reverence here for joggers or teenagers just out from school — just a space, a path, a journey that needs to be made over a space in the way; but, perhaps, not even in the way, simply ignored.

Let's leave our isolation and get back to the path. Make a left at the next junction. Do you see that? Straight ahead? It's a ruin in the midst of refurbishment: the oldest dissenter chapel in Europe. Walk towards it.

In the clearing at the top of the chapel, above the nave, is an old tree, right here on your right. Do you see? It has a sign announcing that it has survived two fires. Not ten feet away is a burnt out fire site with ash. Perhaps this site has some ritualistic significance for people. They can't seem to resist lighting fires here. Or perhaps the sign declaring the tree's survival inspires people to continue the tradition. Or maybe all this is just a coincidence. Let's sit here. The sun is nice. No need for a fire.

5. Teleconnection Teledirection

An urban game for two pedestrian players

Equipment:
Two mobile phones.

Rules:
Begin back to back, phone in hand.

The leader explores the city in any direction, and at whatever pace, they choose.

Every time the leader turns left or right, doubles back, pauses or resumes their walk, they text this direction to the follower.

The follower may only act when following instructions from the leader.

The role of leader is swapped every 15 minutes.

Neither follower nor leader may enter any building.

I CANNOT SEE THE SUMMIT FROM HERE

I 'claimed' not climbed an area of approximately 5 kilometers by 2 kilometers with 20 burns that make up the area and empty themselves into the Water of Nevis. I reflected on my own feelings of discovering and owning this landscape, the entirety of this upland space. I wandered for a day as an Outlandian* out and out into and around the Water of Nevis, East of Steall ruins, with An Gearanach (982 m) and Binnein Beag (943 m) and Binnein Mor (1130 m) to the south and Aonach Beag (1234 m) to the north. I realised as I 'contoured' what was becoming my own upland space that my approach to walking; wandering along the maps contours, sometimes taking bearings to 'kinks' in the contour lines, and then wandering off course away from the paths that this was my preferred way of navigating and walking my way through any mountainous area. On days when there is no need to get anywhere in particular and in June, with long periods of day-light, this is much easier to do. Just pick a site, as I did here, between the Water of Nevis, Allt Coire nan Laogh, and Tom an Eite, Abhainn Rath and take yourself 'Contouring' for a day. I walked between most of the streams in an area of five by two kilometers. Sitting, crouching and cowering in 'my' landscape, down and up close to the water, hidden from view.

Foot Notes

*In 2013 I was a residency artist for one week at Outlandia. Alec Finlay, artist and poet described me as an OUTLANDIAN. Outlandia is a London Fieldwork's project which is an off grid tree house artist studio and field-station in Glen Nevis, Lochabar, Scotland. The residency was organised by London Fieldworks.

Interruption... **Walking and Ruination – or what it means to keep a secret**

In 2004 – it was at Easter – I wrote a short article entitled '25 Instructions For Performance in Cities' (2005) while somewhat incongruously crossing the English Channel in a ferry on what was ostensibly a 'booze cruise'. The article was inspired by what was, in those days at least, a somewhat hermetic area of research and practice, but which has now expanded to become a field in its own right: walking and performance. In this respect, then, this short article, the one I am writing in Glasgow in February 2015, might perhaps be approached as a kind of ghost walk, a walk backwards in time to a topic, that while it still continues to inform my research, has accumulated traction, aggregated different meanings and inflections, and entangled itself in a whole lattice work of competing and often contradictory methodologies and concepts. Indeed, we might say that my relationship to walking has weathered, become, in a sense, a mirror image of the concrete or asphalt upon which so many of my walks were 'performed' in Leicester, Lancaster and Aberystwyth in the intervening years.

All fifty or so contributions to this volume exemplify in the most axiomatic of ways that there is no simple method for walking or indeed for describing a walk. Like a performance score, a walk is an open-ended phenomenon, no one knows in advance what will present itself or who you might meet. The meaning is in the doing, properly performative then, which is to say, self-generating, contingent, improvisatory, light-footed and rooted in the everyday. It is also unexpected. On the route of my daily walk along the Forth and Clyde canal in Glasgow, I am sometimes astonished as I watch brown bottles of empty Buckfast Tonic Wine gleam in the water, to see a huge, looming brutalist tower-block rise up and attack the corner of my eyeball. To walk is to montage, to assemble difference, to exist as a kind of mad, avant-garde camera eye, the socket discombobulating, rendered insane by vision itself.

There is also a high possibility of failure; that the performance of the score or walk (or both, if that is the instruction, as it is in some of the examples in this volume) might not amount to much. A favourite building might have been destroyed, a path re-routed, a neighbourhood gentrified, perhaps even, as has happened in Wales, a village flooded or requisitioned by the state. We are in Proustian territory here, but with a difference – minor key Proust. This is not the famous Proust of the madeleine, the Marcel who is able through the sensory play of the *mémoire involuntaire* to recover, like Henri Bergson, lost time (*le temps perdu*) in the present. Rather this is the Proust of failure, the absurd Proust, the one for whom lost time is wasted time, impossible, irrecoverable, out of reach. Consider, for instance, the tragicomic potential of the passage below:

> And so it is with our own past. It is a labour in vain to attempt to recapture it all: all the efforts of our intellect must prove futile. The past is hidden somewhere outside the realm, beyond the reach of intellect, in some material object (in the sensation which that material object will give us) of which we have no inkling. And it depends on chance whether or not we have come upon this object before we ourselves must die. (Proust 1984: 47-8)

What I love about this writing, and this is certainly what also seduces me in Robert Walser's horrific and shocking short story 'The Walk' (1917), is the idea of chance, the sense in which there is no guarantee that we will ever keep our appointment with the past, that it all might have happened without us. Perhaps it's me, but I find great consolation in the image of someone walking past, blithely and without noticing, the redemptive object that will allow access to one's secret life. Was this, I wonder, what Samuel Beckett thought when wandering the streets of South West London, again and again, as he tried to incorporate the shock waves of his psychoanalytical sessions with Wilfrid Bion at the Tavistock clinic in the winter of 1934? In 1930, Beckett had published *Proust,* a proto-absurdist account of Proust's writing, in which all hope of redemptive memory is banished in advance and replaced, instead, with a Schopenhauerian will to negation.

Some of my friends, including my colleague Dee Heddon and Wrights & Sites, like to walk in groups, I, on the other hand, always prefer to walk alone. Though fully aware that my gender and 'able-bodiedness' assign me special privilege, I walk in order to think, to engage in a kind of embodied writing, to let an idea, like a landscape, unfold. I have always found that difficult to do in company, and am willing to wager that this is how I will engage with the walks listed in this book when it appears. There is nothing exclusive or regulatory in this strategy. Other users will doubtless have different ideas and practices of engagement.

Much has been written about the intimate, perhaps even symbiotic relationship that exists between walking and thinking. One thinks here, of course, of Immanuel Kant heading out for his daily constitutional through the streets and fields of Königsberg as he composed his tripartite series of *Critiques* between 1780 and 1790; or of Walter Benjamin, in the 1930s separated from his son and always on the verge of homelessness, pacing through the I and II Arrondissements in Paris on the lookout for remnants – 'fossils' he called them - of the arcades or 'dream palaces' that were so popular in this area of the city in the nineteenth century. Likewise, Friedrich Nietzsche cautioned, in typically melodramatic fashion, that he never trusted a thought that came to him while indoors; and more recently, Rebecca Solnit, in her classic study *Wanderlust : A Short History of Walking* (2001), has argued that 3 mph is the classic pace for thinking.

With her invitation to write this preamble, Claire Hind sent this citation from Eric Anthamatten's 'Philosophy begins with Wander':

> Philosophy begins with wonder (*thanmazein*). To riff with a homophone 'Philosophy begins with wander'. It is precisely the wandering that facilitates the wondering, and the philosopher wonders while he wanders. The structure of thought is not a straight line, but a wandering, an ambling, a meandering, a walkabout. The dialectic zings, zags, not aimlessly, but less characterised by a straight line than a squiggle that goes this way, then that, moves forward, then turns back on itself. Philosophy is just this movement. (2012: 13)

In two articles, '*Mourning Walk* and Pedestrian Performance: History, Aesthetics and Ethics' (2009) and '*Pas de Deux*' (with Nicolas Whybrow), I tried to advance my own theory for this mysterious connection between walking and philosophy by drawing, first, on ideas of cinema, and second, on the technical vocabulary of versification that creates a distinct analogy between the beat of a line and the beat of a foot.[1] Increasingly, however, I am minded to think of the relationship between walking and thinking (and I use that word to encompass making), in terms of a creative process of ruination, which troubles normative notions of the archive. It is surely no coincidence that in French, the word for step or pace (*un pas*) has a negative sense when used in syntactical construction such as 'Je ne vois pas' or 'Je ne suis pas'. In this example of what linguists call 'sentential negation', the step (*le pas*) is something that erases what came before it, making the past dissolve in the dust, wiping away, we might say, all traces of self-presence. This negative, essentially forward-looking significance of walking is seen, too, in the French self-reflexive verb *se promener*, which translates, literally as 'to take oneself for a walk'. The prefix of *se promener*, in this instance, rooted, as it is, in the Latin *pro* (to go forth), assigns an essentially projective significance to walking, as if everything you are, and ever were, was somehow always being placed in crisis. The negativity of the step *(le pas)* moving relentlessly into the future, is willing to wager on loss, and to accept that nothing can be predicted in advance

How different such a process of negation is from the current obsession with archiving, which as Jacques Derrida has suggested in *Mal d'archive: une impression freudienne* (*Archive Fever: A Freudian Impression*) is a kind of 'infinity of evil' (1998: 20-1). Unlike the score or the walk, the archive, as Derrida explains it, always tries to impose an order, to invest in an act of authentic conservation, in which the past will somehow be able to transcend the vagaries, fictions and fragilities of memory. Whereas the archive, in its most normative form, seeks

---

[1] See also John Hall's wonderful rumination on walking and prosody, 'Foot, Mouth and Ear: Some thoughts on prosody and performance' (2012).

to control the past by fixing it in a prosthetic of sorts (a tablet, page, floppy disk, or electronic cloud), walking, when conceived as an act of necessary negation, reduces the past to ashes, to cinders. So that while the trace of my footprint might remain, my other foot is always rising into the air, willing to move on, to become something different, something new. At the very end of *Archive Fever*, Derrida, while sitting on the slopes of Mount Vesuvius, makes this statement:

> [O]f the secret itself, there can be no archive, by definition. The secret is the very ash of the archive, the place where it no longer even makes sense to say 'the very ash' (*la cendre même*) or 'right on the ash' (*à même la cendre*). There is no sense in searching for the secret of what anyone may have known. (1998: 100)

Inevitably, perhaps, in light what I have been arguing, I cannot help but see walking (again) as a kind of secret.[2] Of course the trace or impress of the foot remains, but what can we say of the living, singular person who makes those marks with a step (*un pas*) which is always a negation? Instead of approaching this negation as a melancholic reminder of what was, characterised by an impossible drive to make the secret speak – the logic of the archive as a logic of historical truth, in other words – I wonder if it might make more sense to celebrate walking as an act of perpetual and incessant ruination, an instance of a secret that refuses, stubbornly, to reveal itself? Faced with this secret, the one who remains, be that a reader or maker of performance, is constrained to respond to the footprint in a different way, to use the secret not as a sign of truth, but as a catalyst of/for imagining, a type of speculation, then, that avoids the mistake of Orpheus. Here the point is not to look back to the past but to keep one's eye firmly on what is ahead, in affirming, that is, the future, which is tantamount to affirming the impersonal flux and flow of a time that we can never inhabit fully or know.

---

[2] I use the word again here as I have written quite extensively on the secret in my article, '*Mourning Walk* and Pedestrian Performance: History, Aesthetics and Ethics' (2009: 53).

To turn from philosophy to performance practice, such an affirmation is consonant with the logic of the score, those '25 Instructions for Performance in Cities' that I proposed a decade or so ago, and which has, in some small way, acted a stimulus for this volume. To perform a score is not to perform in the name of truth, as if one were somehow concerned with idealising a perfect, self-contained actualisation of the original instruction; rather, it is to affirm the necessity of betrayal and the ineluctable reality of failure. In this way, through the necessary ruination of the instruction, the performed score, like the walk, is a guardian of the secret. It realises that the footprints it leaves are a kind of wreckage, an act of creative destruction that has the generosity to foreclose in advance its own will to truth, to temper its own archive fever, and to leave a space for ghosts of the future to come, those spectres who are always still to arrive but yet are strangely already here.

References

Anthamatten, Eric (2012), 'Philosophy begins with Wander', *Nomadic Sojourns,* 1:1

Derrida, Jacques (1998), *Archive Fever: A Freudian Impression*, trans. Eric Prenowitz, University of Chicago Press

Hall, John (2012), 'Foot, Mouth and Ear: Some thoughts on prosody and performance', *Performance Research*: 'On Foot', 17:2, 36:41

Lavery, Carl (2005), '25 Instructions for Performance in Cities', *Studies in Theatre and Performance*, 25:3, 229-38

Lavery, Carl (2009), '*Mourning Walk* and Pedestrian Performance: History, Aesthetics and Ethics' in Roberta Mock (ed.), *Walking, Writing and Performance: Autobiographical Texts by Deirdre Heddon, Carl Lavery and Phil Smith,* Intellect, pp. 41-56

Lavery, Carl and Nicolas Whybrow (2012), '*Pas de Deux*', *Performance Research*: 'On Foot', 17:2, 1-11

Proust, Marcel (1984), *Remembrance of Things Past, vol 1*, trans C. K. Scott Moncrieff and Terence Kilmartin, Penguin

Exchange clipboards. Repeat, as above: adding onto the last line the other wrote, thus building a collabo

7.

Off-the-Grid Walking cARTography:
A Mother/Daughter Poetics of Place Collaboration
…Bronwyn Preece and Similkameen O'Rourke (11 yrs)…

Location: Lasqueti Island, British Columbia, Canada

Pacing This Place…

The beginning is dark, yet light
Green and brown twisting trees
The little shacks in the woods are almost hidden.
Shadows and sun dance patterns, rimmed with
Fallen umber leaves…alder, maple…wrapping
Around roots of cedar, yew, and boulder…
Colourful kids on bikes come by
The banks of oh-so-rich, brown dirt
Moss is so moist at this time of year
And the distant bass beat from a musical home
Wafts over long-forgotten, stashed-in-woods vehicles
But nothing dampens the amphibian symphony.
Lucky beer cans are here, even though we're off-the-grid.
People like to party, but there is no excuse for trash.
10 people could hold hands around this tree
Or more. Or less. Numbers, people, place merge
Even with the reminder of a single brightly painted car.
A wave acknowledges volumes as we breathe together this space.
Glittering sunshine shines into the brook,
Even though the brook is deep, the grass still grows.
You have no idea how much my feet hurt right now.
Soleful/Soul-full reminders of constant contact
Ground, Earth, Sky, Leaves, Me, You, Us, Lasqueti
The boundaries are blurred and oddly present still.
The little "wee" pond is lovely
With the chirp of bird
I love it.
Then…a driftwood gate with a bell
Sun splashes through alder
And a telephone box: #141
The road ends really abruptly!
I am grateful for this journey
WE ARE HERE!

Previously published in Performing Motherhood (Demeter Press, 2014). Reproduced with permission.

rative poem of place…merging and marking perspectives of age and experience. 7. Spend six hours (in half hour increments) walking, talking, and creating together.…

etry in response to this place. Fold the paper over, leaving the final line exposed. 6. Set timer to go off in 30 minutes. Start walking. In half an hour, when timer goes off, stop.

Road. 5. Begin: Each take three photos of this place. Each, on a respective clipboard, write three lines of po

8. Going in Circles

Circumambulation is one of the most spiritual walking practices there is. Circles are probably the most spiritual shape, a symbol of the infinite, the emptiness but simultaneously the whole. Most major religions practice some form of circumambulation for its spiritual significance.

Circles are also the most natural shape: planets, eggs, water-droplets, etc. all fall naturally into round shapes. Not to mention life cycles.

If walking, as I have always maintained, is the best form of travel for observation, then walking again and again round an object is even more significant. Circling an object creates a bond with it, and with each pass a new detail is noticed.

In my own circumambulations I find I enter a meditative and therapeutic mindset but am also hyper aware of my surroundings. Going round and round I notice every detail and also hear more, tuning into this place and time. I circle into a mindset that is spiritual, meditative and induces inspiration.

The object you move around must be something revered or something you wish to investigate. Moving around it you pay homage, reverence, show a willingness to learn it intimately.

For a truly significant experience with the human soul, find an object of some importance to you and then circle to gain a connection to it that is both intimate and spiritual.

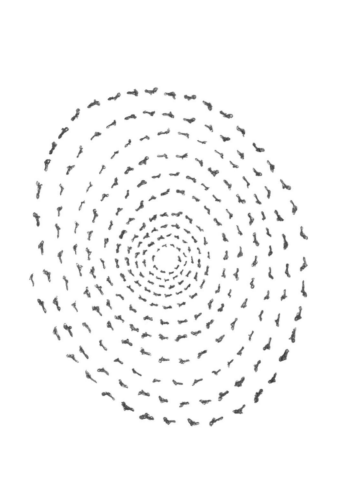

walk with me
with –

seeds in your hair; burs on your clothes
stones in your pocket

the smell of the sea on your skin
your nails painted the colour of the sky

flutter around light   (infatuated moth)

I   you cannot dream
II   the stars call your name
III   poetry is your religion

walk with me
when –

the last desiccated leaf has married
the swollen river
the trees whisper as they sway
the first wren sings

you are blindfold   (where is your
sense of direction now?)
you stand still to keep moving

walk with me
when –

the hole is your shoe lets the light in
you are naked, though your clothes
drape in many layers

the earth hums and you hum back
night turns to day
 (the morning
seems as long
as the world
is old)

you cannot see a future
(entrenched in your past)

VII   asleep
VIII   [having eaten larks tongues
you grown wings]
IX   take timid steps

the horizon is a concept of disbelief
you know not earth from sky

a constellation of freckles
(across the bridge of your nose)

the encumbered
the abandoned
the reckless

IV   your mouth is open;
you taste the air
V   your ears are closed
(remain in
another world)
VI   your arms are raised;
you close your eyes
to the heavens

walk with me
when –

tears in your eyes distort your view
our eyes are not able to meet

my hand is in your hand
breath is one

the sky is a clot of blood
the morning is golden and the air sparkles
the moon scintillates across still waters

our lives –
fragile pathways

10. The Underpass

Many of London's 'multi-exit' pedestrian underpasses are clearly signed for your walking convenience. Many conform to a graphical standard that indicates all the exits by number, on a very small-scale map of the local area. Tube stations often deploy similar signage and it is possible to generate walks of your own from these numbering systems, should you value chance and gameplay over utility and purpose.

Method (note: you will need a coin)

1. Find an entrance/exit and an exit map to ascertain the number of the exit that you have chosen, for example 5.

2. Look for the highest number on the exit map, for example 7.

3. Subtract the lowest from the highest number.

4. Head for the exit with the resultant number. This gets you started, etc.

Previously published by Ellipsis London (2000) and online at http://bit.ly/londonwalking – reproduced with the author's permission.

11. Maternity Leaves

Take a walk, just to get out of the house.
Take the bag and pushchair and raincover and whatnot.

Take stock of who you have become.

Take my word for it — it gets easier than this.

Take the same route you always take.
Take note of the details of the season.
Take a look at your companion in the pushchair.
Take pleasure in the changes in both since last time.

Take in this moment.

Take a picture to remember it by.
Take a few steps further from the pushchair than is emotionally comfortable.
Take a risk and take one more step.
Take no notice of the real or imagined reactions of passers-by.
Take the opportunity to repeat the above whenever you can.

Take care, though.

Take care.

For the first year of my daughter's life, I photographed a series of short performative walks within a one-mile radius of my home, exploring the time and space of motherhood. Drifting around my own locality, I discovered that my newly myopic attention to the patterns, demographics, and waymarkers paralleled that which is given to newborns. The slow changing of the seasons similarly reminded me that I couldn't will her to smile, not have colic, sleep all night, eat solids, walk, etc. any faster than nature intended.

Like Rousseau, these (not quite) solitary walks offered me precious time for reverie, but also to reflect on my choice to become a mother. In addition to the themes of ambivalence and abandonment, I intended to document a performer interrogating her own performance in this new role, as I dared myself to take a few more steps away from my subject/audience/co-performer than was emotionally comfortable. This exploration of distance was subtly affected by the real and imagined judgements of passers-by, and so I titled the images by detailing the number of steps taken in plaintive acknowledgement of my responsibility. The difference between 'ahh, look — a mother taking a photo of her baby' and 'what the hell is she doing?' is only a few paces.

12. Perambulator

Map the area that you live in (or walk regularly in) for pram/pushchair/buggy/stroller use - where are the awkward spots?

Steps? Narrow pavements? No pavements? Steep kerbs? Railings? Cars parked in the way?

Create a walking route that highlights these problematic spots.

Invite other pram users to walk with you, create a **Perambulator Parade** collectively performing the sites of awkwardness. Help one another over and around the obstacles.

Optional follow-on task:

Choose one (or more) of the awkward spots and try to get it fixed. If it's on a public path write to the council, invite a local councillor to do the **Perambulator** walk with you, show them the problem and ask them to sort it out. If the problem spot belongs to a business or other organisation contact them and ask them to fix it — send pictures of the **Perambulator** performance of overcoming the obstacle.

13. Walking In Drains

Our late modern living arrangement relies upon infrastructure that includes sophisticated urban drainage systems. Artificial pipes and cavities are needed to direct sewer waste from homes, schools and businesses, etc. as well as stormwater runoff from roads, roofs, pathways and other impervious or hard surfaces. Older drains across the UK and Europe are combined systems, meaning that they collect stormwater and sanitary sewage. In Melbourne, Australia, we have a vast drainage network that is dedicated to stormwater runoff. Many of the stormwater drains are big enough to walk through and they can reach out for kilometres underneath the busy streets of the metropolis; it is throughout these sub-suburban spaces that my walking, as a creative cultural practice, takes place (fine weather permitting).

The word 'drain' carries abject connotations; perhaps I'm polymorphously perverse to find drains, and urban exploration in general, incredibly alluring — a feast for the scopophilic gaze. Of course, I still experience a kind of industrialised romanticism when I am walking through a century-old space with my torch and stop for a moment to admire a beautiful bluestone tunnel, or to appreciate how closely the stormwater resembles liquid crystal as it trickles along the red brick floor. As a form of critical praxis, however, walking in drains is a way for me to transgress the rigid structures of the city that routinely discipline our bodies, in turn shaping how we communicate with each other.

TASK :	Hail the Subterranean
Duration:	about 2 to 3 minutes
Props:	none
Effect:	defamiliarising

Next time you are walking through your suburb or city, day or night, it's entirely possible that someone will be passing by beneath your feet. If you see a gutter box along the side of the road, peer into it; a side-pipe could lead to a larger tunnel. If you can see a side-pipe, kneel down beside the gutter and position your mouth near the cavity. Risk attracting sideways glances from street-level pedestrians by calling 'Hello'" once or twice into the gutter box. Remain quiet for a few moments; listen. Perhaps a friendly voice will greet you back.

14. Notes to the novice pedestrian

Upon arrival at your chosen street (presumably by train or bus or car or bike), take a moment to observe the actions of your (now) fellow pedestrians. At first the smooth passage of the crowds may seem an unlikely achievement. Look a while longer and you'll notice the passage is patterned. You will begin to notice the work that your fellow pedestrians do to bring those patterns into being. This is an essential noticing for the novice pedestrian. But let us not get ahead of ourselves. We must walk before we can run.

You will notice people forming themselves, on your street, in to files, moving queues, of sorts. Not rigidly so, but recognisably enough. Choose a direction. Go with the flow. Adjust your pace to loosely fall in with those around you. Too fast and people will wonder what it is you're up to. Too slow and you're an obstacle. Be sure to plan ahead and cooperate with those around you to negotiate objects such as benches, bins and bollards.

Make eye contact with your fellow pedestrians. People walking in the opposite direction cannot read your intentions (experienced pedestrians are adept at this) if you do not. Glance, do not stare; recognise people as persons, but do not make them the object of special attention or scrutiny.

Take care to never match directly the pace of a stranger walking next to you. That way organisational trouble lies. Onlookers will assume you are together (matched pace is reserved for 'withs') and it will force that person to speed up or slow down to signal to all that you are not.

At the same time, keep an eye out for actual withs. They are sometimes easy to spot — a couple holding hands, say — but sometimes they can extend across a street in ways that are hard (for the novice) to see. Walking straight through withs requires advanced techniques and is probably best avoided.

Walking in cities is hard work, but the best way to learn is by doing. It will soon feel completely effortless.

From: Clare Qualmann (c.qualmann)

Sent: 24 May 2014 13:29
To: Claire Hind (C.Hind)
Subject: Re: Ways to Wander project

Dear Claire,

Reading about your memories of walking in Wales reminds me of when Dee Heddon interviewed me for the *Walking Women* project a few years ago. She had asked me if I'd done leisure walking, or hiking, as a child, and I had said no. A couple of hours later at home I'd reflected on this response, and had to email her and explain that it was totally untrue - that my childhood was full of walks, long muddy freezing cold rainy walks (much of the time) but also very beautiful - and as you describe - oft repeated walks. The coastal paths of Cornwall spring to mind - we were the family looking under equipped with at least one of us wearing flip-flops, or trying to push a pushchair, or using an umbrella to try and shelter from the rain on the cliff top, being frowned upon by serious hikers in waterproofs with maps around their necks. A few days later I also remembered that I'd done some longer distance walks on my own as a teenager - the Tinner's Way in Cornwall for example.

On reflection I think my reflex response related to my walking work; in my art practice I'm much more interested in everyday walks (which in my adult life has always meant urban) than long distance, leisure, and rural walks (though I still like these as leisure activities).

Clare

15.

Thank you for reading this text
It contains instructions for a walk
Please perform each action before reading the line that follows it
Leave the building via the front entrance and turn left
Stop to tie your shoelace (if you don't have laces pretend you do)
Look behind you to check you are not being followed
Head in the direction of the water
Be careful not to tread in the dog shit
Tune in to the sound of the birdsong
Adopt the walk of a fellow pedestrian
Consider the traces you are collecting
Consider the traces you are leaving
When you reach the water slow down and stop at the edge
Stand facing the water for a few moments
Imagine the water is no more than an inch deep

16. Following Forgotten Footprints

Return to your old hunting ground and choose a path you used as a child or a few years back. Using the following words, note how things return to walk once more along your paths of memory. You may use photography, drawing, writing or video to document your walk, or you may just experience it. Back home you might walk up to the attic in an attempt to continue your walk along the trails of reminiscence. Boxes full of childhood treasures or pictures of places long forgotten may compare to your new experience of these same sites. It is up to you to create a new walk which reveals the stratified trail you have followed.

Search	Scrutiny	Trees
Listen	Pursue	The attic
The soil	Chase	Photograph
Rummage	The air	Road
Learn	The ground	Recognise
Stones	Faces	Tracks
Recall	Climb	Scent
Look	Voices	Route
Find	Earth	Beaten track
Clouds	Untangle	Footsteps
Follow	The trail	Sky
Story	Smells	Mark
The wall	Memorise	Walk
Track	Remember	Experience
Hunt	Unfold	The line
Explore	Noises	Count
Call up	The house	Leaves
Go	Open	Night
See	Feel	Path
Investigate	Dark	Undergrowth

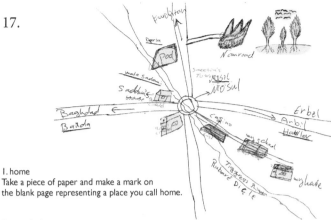

1. home
Take a piece of paper and make a mark on
the blank page representing a place you call home.

2. special place
Think of a place nearby your home that is special to you, perhaps a place you have
made many journeys to. Map the way from the threshold of your home to this special place.

3. landmarks
Mark the landmarks that are along the way from your home to this special place.
These may be features which mark locations of significant events and details of your own
personal history.

4. unfamiliar place
Go somewhere unfamiliar or different to the home you have mapped and take a walk there
using your original map as a guide through this place.

Start walking and use a piece of tracing paper to mark the landmarks you see along the way
over those on your original map until you arrive at your special place.

5. along the way
As you walk follow the 'steps' below marking a response on your tracing paper.

> step
> Stop at a place where something reminds you of the home.
> What details in this place remind you of that place?
> What could you do here that would make you feel at home?

> step
> Stop at a place that is unfamiliar to you. How does this place make you feel?
> What object would you put in this landscape to make it more familiar?

> step
> Stop at a place that is familiar to you. How is it familiar?

> step
> Stop at a place you find fascinating or comforting along your walk.
> What interests you or draws your attention to this place.

6. last step
When you find your special place and arrive at the end of your walk mark this place and
rename it.

18. STEP-BY-STEP

STEP BY STEP:

Here

notate/draw/map your sequences
across each of the four cards
available.

1/4

Challenge yourself to keep your
eyes shut whilst walking. PACE
around something or someone. Place
your toes in CONTACT with the floor
first.

Follow: lines/your nose/sounds/yellow

small sequences

2/4

Walk as SLOW as you dare. FEEL
your SKIN against your clothes as
you MOVE. Step with an irregular
rhythm.

Cross: your legs / the road / a
threshold / _____

for the city

3/4

Walk BACKWARDS looking at the
SKY. Walk FORWARDS looking at the
ground. Keep changing the length of
your STRIDE.

Repeat: with gusto / a sound you heard
/ _____ / _____

There

neilandsimone.co.uk

4/4

Walk like a STRANGER, take on their
gait. BLINK three times for every
step you take. Stop. Be STILL.
OBSERVE people walking around you.

Focus: on your breath / _____ /
_____ / _____

Try one step at a time or any combination of
the above.
Nottdance Festival 2013   www.dance4.co.uk

19. City Centre

Cities tend to start in the middle and spread outwards, thinning as they go. Most of us know this journey. There is a familiar phenomenology of departure: leaving the centre behind, perhaps heading for home, the built environment starts to slacken off and the skyline opens out; the compacted intricacy of the streets unravels; the density of traffic eases and inching progress gives way to longer surges of movement (if you are in a taxi or on a bus, that is); the barrage of advertising and signage falls off; the noise drops a notch or two, perhaps a certain tension too. None of this is uniform; the geography of most cities is too complex for that. Headed the other way, the city gathers itself together again and the scale of things shifts upwards until at some point we can say we are more or less back in the middle of things. But where is that exactly, and how can we be sure?

Why not try this out? If you are in the middle of a city, walk away from it. Keep going. Ask yourself, as you go, 'How do I know I'm leaving it behind?' 'What is there less or more of; what has dropped away or become apparent; what has changed? Mind how you go. Being 'not from round here' might mean something different in the middle of things (where it applies to almost everyone) than it does as you move towards the edges. Had enough? Change direction and head back 'in'. No need to retrace your steps if you don't want to. Just follow your nose. You can do it. There will be all sorts of cues and indications, an accumulating body of evidence *en route* that you are getting there. But where? This question can be answered sideways. Among the more explicit indications you might come across as you make your way (back) in will be signs pointing the way, like this:

CITY CENTRE

But you are unlikely to encounter a sign telling you that you have arrived. This is, of course, one of the surest indications available that you are back in the middle of things: the signs pointing the way will have dried up.

Play the City Now or Never!

Take a seat: smile at your neighbour

Use something (or someone) to help you balance for 10 seconds

Find a line to follow: face the future

Seek a green patch: enjoy it while it lasts

Close your eyes: listen to the city passing you by

Place your hands on an old building: caress the past

1. cut out
2. assemble
3. play!

Idit Elia Nathan & Helen Stratford © 2013

cut here

cut between scissors only

- - - - fold here
(away from you)

cut here

21. Walking with my Dog

So turn right out of my gate down to the end of the street, 30 seconds if you're on your own but 3 or 4 minutes with the dog. And you are with the dog. I should say right now you need to get the clock out of your head: he walks slowly and stops frequently to sniff and to let his back legs catch up with the front. There is a corner here which he stands at to avoid a sharp right turn onto a steep bit of road. If you pull he will resist. He will sit down. He will outwait you. Relax and remember patience.

Cross the road, turn left into the lane which runs past the allotments and the small-holding with goats, ponies and geese. If you have remembered to bring an apple, feed the livestock. Continue on this lane to the park. Now you can take him off the lead. Walk on and he will follow at his own pace. He is as concerned about losing you as you are about losing him. He likes to keep his distance about 10 feet behind you. If you stop, thinking he'll catch up with you, he stops too. Meeting other dogs, you never know what he'll do, make friends or have a go. He's better off the lead.

Cross the slab bridge onto the left bank of the beck, give the ducks a wide berth and reach your turning point at the stone bridge. Here he likes to get to the middle and stand still. I don't know why, maybe he's just having a rest.

By the time you start home you are both in a rhythm. His legs have warmed up, he starts to walk better and you start to drift off with your thoughts; singing, enjoying the trees, rehearsing that thing you want to say to someone but probably never will. And then you come back to him. He is old and I don't know how much longer he'll be around. So make the most, let him take his time and learn to take yours.

[Postscript: sadly, my dog Rufus died on 12th December 2014. He loved the park.]

22.

Walk as you think an octopus thinks.

Look ahead with the eye of driftwood.

Let another moving thing, a wave or a spider, take away something bad.

As you go, touch everything.

Walk slowly, leave no mark but that one, you know...

Be still for ten minutes.

Collect a hundred of something.

Throw a stone into water. Imagine the ripples magnified tenfold. Walk the difficult shape where the tenth ripple dissipated.

For a mile, roll a stick in front of you.

Decorate a stick and carry it.

Pick up two stones and clap them together to the metre of your walk.

Think of a different sea every step.

Use your whole body to leave a trace.

Plan a future walk.

Walk with a friend and take it in turns to carry each other. Hold hands. Make a ritual without discussion.

Give a name to objects you encounter. Every few minutes speak a list of those things. Stop if you forget one and begin the whole thing again. When does this thing end? Let things decide.

Utilise whatever you can find to dig as deep a hole as possible in one hour. Then fill it in. It's not the same. Never go back there again.

Look for your name in street signs.

Spill. Spill it on the road. Spill your guts. Spill the deepest feelings in the smallest spaces. Find companions with whom you can spill intensely. Overthrow the Spill Corporation. Infiltrate the... you know. Sell spill. Swap swill. Parade until you reach the foot of the hill. Walk the marks of your spills upon it. Assume responsibility for every stain, map them; walk the stains in your imagination. Map them while in the bath. While in the public eye. Fight spill, re-direct spill, recycle spill, move spill on to new things. Be spilled, finally.

Lie on your back and memorise the clouds. Under a cloudless sky go blank.

Identify a point half a mile away; as you walk to it compose a poem about what you're going through. On arriving, recite the poem.

Long Shore Drift

```
Carry a
    {stone}
        from
            one
                beach
                    to
                        the
                            next
                                along
                                    the
                                        coast →
```

← drift – longshore – local – of – direction – the – in – walking ←

```
Place the
    {stone}
            on
                the
                    next
                        beach
                            and
                                pick
                                    up
                                        another
                                            one →
```

← there – stone –the – placing – beach – first – the – to – return ←

A (lengthwise) homage to Richard Long's (crosswise) *Crossing Stones* (1987) www.richardlong.org

Part of *Long Shore Drift {Box} pSychogeography for the pSeapSide or 20 ways to wander on the beach* a series of walks devised on a month-long walking retreat in Aberystwyth, Spring 2014. (Purchased at auction by Jane Lloyd Francis, reproduced with permission.)

24. *Walker*

This suggested activity will, I hope, inspire thought about the past practices of walking in your location. Walking is a spatial activity, and one that happens over time. The time frame for a walk encompasses all those who have walked in that place in the past, and all those who will take the same route in the future.

There are three approaches to the *Walker* walk outlined here:

1. Find a phone directory for the area where you are going to walk, and look up 'Walker' in the listings. Using a map, locate as many of those 'Walker' addresses in your area as you can, and set out on foot to visit them.

2. Using a printed map of the city or town where you live, find any 'Walker' Streets, Roads, Walks, Avenues, Drives, Boulevards, Terraces, Courts or Crescents, and walk to as many of them as you can.

3. Walk to a cemetery in your town or city, and walk through it, looking for as many tombstones with the family name 'Walker' on them as you can. It was while doing such a walk many years ago that I found the tombstone for *Corona I. Walker* ('crown' of the walker) in my neighbourhood in Dartmouth, Nova Scotia.

25. The Closer Walk

There is the sidewalk, and you are walking in the middle. There is the path, and you are walking in the middle. Shift your route. Start a new way by walking closer. Walk close to the walls, facades, hedges, fences. Walk as close as you can without touching them. Do it around a house, around a block, along a road. Do it at places you think you already know. Do it at places you want to get to know.

From: Claire Hind (C.Hind)
Sent: 14 September 2014 09:06
To: Clare Qualmann (c.qualmann)
Subject: Re: Ways to Wander project

Dear Clare,

After our conversation on being influenced by Lavery's *25 Instructions for Performance in Cities*, and from your interest in developing a call for this project, I pondered the word 'wander' as an alternative word for walking (nothing new of course in relation to the history and cultures of walking) but in the context of a series of artistic projects the word seemed to suit the call more and more. I was influenced by Anthamatten's idea in 'Philosophy begins with Wander' that 'the structure of thought is not a straight line, but a wandering, an ambling, a meandering, a walkabout. The dialectic zigs, zags, not aimlessly, but less characterized by a straight line than a squiggle that goes this way, then that, moves forward and then turns back on itself'. Curious to know how and what a wander score might look like on a page, I imagined the myriad 'ways' that might shift between free play and rule-based play, or sit somewhere between fluxus scores and ritual encounters, all with their interpretive possibilities. They are all here! Every page is unique. It's so interesting that we have a mixture of wanders that could happen anywhere, with or without rules, some site specific, others designed for our imagination or with an object. These scores remind me of working in the theatre when engaging with the complexities of textual interpretation. Interpreting a Samuel Beckett play, a Caryl Churchill play, and an improvisation task produce diverse and complex differences. If we draw on the rules and stage directions of a Samuel Beckett play, in order to experience them fully we need to *try* to strictly adhere to them and Sara Jane Bailes points out that it is terribly easy to get Beckett's strict instructions "wrong". And how right in another sense - few other theatre works are unequivocal in their directives.

Of course we are not asking for the wanderer to adhere to strict rules for theatrical interpretation. These scores are provocations and our own relationship to the instructions will emerge during the experience. The writing may determine particular rules of engagement with a site, or invite the participant to act in someone's memory, or engage in an imaginative, playful experience. If any of these pages can be lost in translation I would love to see a second edition — with responses from the wanderers to all these lovely ways.

Claire

26. WALKING IDEAS

1) **Get to know a city/town in a different way - especially if you are new to this city.**

   a) You need a wooden spoon.

   b) Decide where to start.

   c) Go there. Stand still and throw the spoon in the air.

   d) One end of this spoon is the pointer finger.

   e) Look where the spoon is pointing and walk in this direction.

   f) Walk till you cannot walk any more (e.g. because of a wall).

   g) Throw the spoon again and walk in the direction it shows.

   h) At each stop look around - look, feel, and so on.

   i) Do not make pictures during your walk! You can draw later.

   j) At some moment you will decide to go back to your starting point. Use a different route. Use the spoon to show the way (but not if it becomes too hard to get back).

2) **Choose a work of art and take it for a walk.** If you like, organise a **Walking Exhibition** and invite others to take part with their artworks.

3) **Make a Walking Sculpture while you walk.**

4) **Walk a poem/tale.**

5) **Walk the gravitational force.**

27. Folding Paper Listening Trumpet

Using earth colours collected in Wales, this hand drawn 'listening trumpet' pattern was made in memory of the geologic layers of slate I saw when I stayed and walked there with members of Footwork in July 2014. What did we hear? Water flowing, sheep bleating, laughter, quiet and loud conversation, footsteps, trains, windmills, a tram, slate thrown into water, voices reverberating on earthen walls, pump clicking/water dripping, people rolling in the grass, and much more.

Print, cut and roll this pattern into a cone, then place tabs in slots to secure. This 'listening trumpet' operates on similar acoustic principles to Beethoven's ear trumpets. Use it on a walk. Stop to listen. The ear acts as the conduit between the outer world and the inner realm of each individual. Aided by the use of these small handmade objects, you may be able to hear and see in alternative ways. Sounds may be subtly amplified and clarified strands of falling water made discrete from one another, the buzz of an insect closer. Invert a trumpet and sight through the large end to the smaller to transform it into a device for locating minute visual phenomena. Play of light and shadow on a patch of moss or lichen may feed a sensory memory bank that accrues as residue of the walk. In experiencing sound as geographical, the process is one of assembling sound into an aural picture of the landscape or urbanspace. The small visual images may likewise be recalled and reassembled.

The sounds and sights of interest on these walks are often so woven into the fabric of the everyday as to be scarcely noticed. Of central concern is recognizing the importance of simple awareness and the resulting enhanced perceptual possibilities. Such activities may filter into our daily lives and yield vivid, though perhaps brief, unexpected experiences. A cultivation of these facilities allows for frequent retreats from the usual patterns of our fast-paced lives and nurtures the human need to break from the mechanical rhythm of contemporary life.

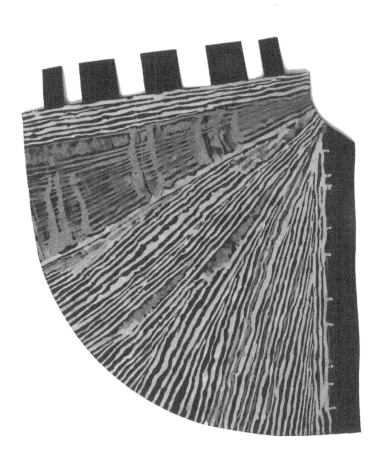

28.

Google the name of your town, city, neighbourhood. Notice where Google plants its pin on the map. Put down your phone and leave all maps behind. Walk to the pin. Create a walking instruction in response to your walk. Share your instruction.

29 The Best of all Possible Places

Wait until 7 am tomorrow morning. If 7 is too early,
wait until half past nine, but do not begin at 8.

Set out with your face to the path of the rising sun
from the central railway, bus or other transit station.

Walk due south at a moderate pace.

Take care to acknowledge passers-by with a
nod of the head. Every third person who passes you
headed in any other direction will be on an
equivalent but opposite path, and might offer useful
instructions. To anyone passing heading in the same
direction at an accelerated pace, click your tongue.

After fifteen minutes have passed without distraction from your
appointed task, select a place to sit. This is the best of all
possible places in at this moment.

30. The A-Game

London is a many-layered city, an impossible shifting mass of briefly overlapping lives all conducted in a spidery street sprawl. Tracing logic and meaning in the streets requires method, and walking is the tool.

The city is full – too full – of walkers, but they are only a certain type making short journeys. Walk alongside and they fall away to be replaced by others, people making their own short trips to offices, shops and schools.

This is where London's main roads come in. The city's skeleton has a series of numbered ribs – A1, A2, A3, A4, A5 – tracing routes that 8 million feet barely touch. They are hostile territory, long, dirty and difficult. The walker feels unwanted, unwelcome, ill-at-ease. The walker needs to know why.

Tracing the routes requires a road map, not an A-Z, showing Greater London in all its trafficked reality, buzzing with vehicles in orbit around the orbital motorway, or pulsing along arterial roads.

The method requires structure, and the road-numbering system provides a clear order to the ancient and remade roads connecting London spokewise:

A1 – the Great North Road, stringing North London together

A2 – a pilgrimage, from the Borough into Kent in the direction of Canterbury, via the Sun-in-the-Sands roundabout

A3 – marching over London Bridge and out through the common spaces of the south west

A4 – a ceremonial route from High Holborn through the Strand and South Kensington to Heathrow and the west

A5 – 10 miles dead straight, Marble Arch to the M1 at Elstree;

A10 – straight as a die, finding flat land all the way through north-east London to the Fens

A12 – the Eastway across Hackney marshes into rural Essex

A13 – a badlands trail, the only A-road with its own literary tradition

Some are missing: no A6, starting at Luton and always a Hertfordshire road; no A7, A8, A9, only to be found in Scotland. But the patterns are clear – walk these roads, into or away from the city, and you will find yourself alone and separate, possessing rare knowledge, knowing what the city may not want you to know.

31. A WALK FOR SEATON CAREW BEACH IN HARTLEPOOL AT LOW TIDE

OBJECTS NEEDED:
1 SHOVEL.
1 COMPASS.

IMAGE: MAXY NEIL BIANCO

INSTRUCTIONS:
START FROM 54° 39' 19.57'' N, 1° 10' 50.29'' W AND WALK NORTH ALONG THE SHORELINE. ON YOUR WAY, YOU ARE MOST LIKELY TO COME ACROSS A GROUP OF SEA-COALERS: STORAGE MEN OF REGIONAL MEMORY. THEY WILL BE SCRAPING SEA-COAL INTO PILES; CREATING RICHARD LONG-ESQUE SPIRALS, AND THEN SHOVELLING THEM ONTO THE BACK OF MODIFIED LAND ROVERS. WHEN YOU SEE THEM, ASK THEM IF THEY NEED A HAND.

32. How to Wander Lonely as a Cloud[3]

The first time you recognised the cloud
brought on by the plague-wind
as distinct as Levanter
           as a Banner   as Lenticular   as Mammato
as storm-filaments, hooked
sky-born skeins
extending into diffluent layered
fleeces, ripped into uncountable numbers . . .
thoughts, seeding themselves . . .
paradoxes, of distinct liquid diameters . . .
you were walking across an open field

caught there between
depths of blue and the purity of white
the rising earth and the horizon, enskied
your mind and memory became grey images.
The Sky Above You (*vaguely* yours): A Pictorial Guide.

Now when you look up you find
the thoughts of others –
unreal colours
unreal truths
the unreality of the world-and-you, speaking

                                                                                e

      are   *right*   *r*   *a*   *t*
We   *all*   *as a*   *s*   *e*
              f   *we go*   *e* *i*   *l*
         our work   *may b*   *n*   *p*
                              s e   *com*
              but it is not fal

                              and it is far better

              far less injurious to   *the mind*

         that   *we*
should be   *little*
         attracted   *to*
                         the   *sky*

---

[3] The performance of this poem will bring the lonely vale and hill walker into the company of Wordsworth, Ruskin, Battan, Ludlam, Scorer, Perrie, Orr, Grant, Turner, Constable, Howard and Tyndall, through the inspiration drawn, and quotation taken from their reflections on clouds.

33. Chip Walk

To be practised in unknown cities (or areas of a city) or any place with potential for multiple chip shops.

1. Locate a chip shop.
2. Buy a bag of chips.
3. Have them wrapped 'open' to eat whilst walking.
4. Choose a direction to walk in.
5. Walk and eat.
6. When you locate another chip shop, repeat from step 2.
7. If you finish your chips before locating another chip shop ask passers-by to point you towards one.
8. Cease when exhausted/sated.

Best practised in a small group (sharing chips) in order to avoid chip poisoning.

Can be adapted to other foodstuffs, depending on local ubiquity.

34.

Walking With Limited Longevity & A Bottle Of Soap Bubbles

Prepare to wander in a big wide-open space where there are no
roads, rivers, cliffs edges, waterfalls or low-flying aircraft

Blow a bubble, watch it go   POP
Blow a bubble and follow its path   POP
Walk with it, run after it, lie underneath it, move with it   POP
Watch it return to follow you
It may even desire to look at you   POP

Desire
      We are going down

Just when you thought you
      had it all planned   out

The wreckage and the ruin   POP

Sensitive, iridescent   POP

Experience the unpredictability of a bubble's journey where there
are no roads, rivers or cliff edges and feel the direction of the wind

Imagine the voice of a man with dark glasses and the voice of an
angel, crying POP ....crying POP   ...cryyyyyyiinnnggg   POP
Fragile. Iridescent. With limited longevity

"I love you even more than I did before, but...".   POP POP POP PO
Wander, imagine, cry and play until your heart stops beating.

35. Walking in a Gallery

Place: Any art gallery showing Douglas Gordon's installation *24 Hour Psycho* (2003).

Work: *24 Hour Psycho* takes Alfred Hitchcock's classic film noir *Psycho* (1960) and slows it down so that it runs (insanely) for 24 hours instead of the original 109 minutes.

Context: Most people spend minutes, if not seconds in front of *24 Hour Psycho*. Perhaps the intensity of the slowness, the sheer concentration required to stick with it, fills them full of horror, provokes some premonition of dread, perhaps even an anticipation of their own death. At any rate, few people seem up to the task.

Qualification: This from Gilles Deleuze:

> 'The truths which intelligence grasps directly in the open light of day have something less profound, less necessary about them than those which life has communicated to us in spite of ourselves in an impression, a material impression because it has reached us through our senses' (1964, p.161).

#Instruction 1: Go to the gallery. Spend 4 hours in front of *24 Hour Psycho*.

#Instruction 2: Resist all attempts to leave the screen; repress all desires to abscond. Give yourself up to the work (this will be impossible, happily).

#Instruction 3: Find a way to walk through *24 Hour Psycho*. Let it walk through you. Become porous. Abandon yourself. Find a new way to breathe.

Reflection: In the fresh air now, on the steps of the gallery, you are exhausted, biochemically altered. Consider what it means to walk standing still, in the steps of a memory, haunted by a heartbeat, a place, a rhythm, that you are still in. In this dislocated state, attune yourself to the pull of gravity, to the weight of the world, to the way in which everything – and everyone – is on the verge of some potential collapse, becoming different, breaking up, dissolving. Exult in the chaos, in the swirl of atoms.

Interrogation: Is there a point at which walking becomes swimming?

Gilles Deleuze, *Proust and Signs*, trans R. Howard (Georges Braziller, 1964).

36. Transecting

You will need: a map, a permanent marker, comfortable footwear.

Transect, *noun*: A line or a belt of land along which a survey is made of the plant or animal life or some other feature.

In 2007 I scrawled the following words across a map of Devon:

If a transect could be nine miles long and still function as such, what would you be sampling? People, place, ecology, a culture, country...to sample that which is truly yours alone, to stroll through your own perception, to explore the labyrinth of your own thought, use the footsteps as a rhythm for the mind and the landscape as a canvas for the imagination.

This transect, a line drawn between my door and Dartmoor, walked regularly, over a given period became *transecting*.

Transecting, *gerund*: Drawing a line between two points on a map; the subsequent attempt to articulate that place through walking, talking or writing it into being.

Draw a line between your current location and another key point: a park, river, shoreline, skyscraper or monument for example. Holding to this line as much as possible, transect the social, historical and personal archives of this transect.

Five starting points for transecting:

1. **North/South.** Walking your transect with a camera and a compass, take a photograph facing north and south every 5 minutes. Collate photographs.
2. **Sky to Soil.** Record an image of the ground beneath your feet and the sky above your head every 5 minutes. Collate images.
3. **Signs of life.** With a notebook and pencil, every 10 minutes write down every sign you can read within sight of the naked eye. Make sure to record nothing if there is nothing.
4. **Tell me about it.** With a notebook and a pencil, every 10 minutes write down two words that describe your current experience.
5. **I think it went like this.** Traverse your transect with no equipment (no camera, no pencil etc, no map). Upon returning try and remember your first step: transcribe your walk from that point on. In list form or narrative, using free association or strict attempts at pure recollection.

37. Radically Walking

This is an invitation to take back the streets, to reclaim what's public by being together.

1. In groups of between two and five go to a place that once was (or felt) public but now is (or feels) private. (These places are easy to find: city squares and parks, tourist destinations, bus, tram, train and tube stations, for example).

2. Walk around the site and talk about what is public space, in a public way.

3. Experiment with prolonging this discussion over an hour, a morning, a whole day.

4. Observe how this walking and talking affected you and others in the space.

5. How have the steps you have taken together altered the text of the site?

The City today is a site that is increasingly privately owned — soon to be completely devoid of 'public' space. The suggestion that globalisation has brought the diverse communities of the world together is a contested one. Arguably, this globalisation has created a globe full of tourists where no one truly belongs anywhere.

38. For the River Valley

For the river valley:

Walk in silence
Consider an invitation to take off your shoes
Follow the path so that you are guided by the footsteps of others
Lift up your head
Listen out for, or look for something *in particular*. A colour? A type of birdsong?
A repeated mark?

Gather
Create a disturbance
Allow the disturbance to subside
Notice any response and return to calm

In pairs: Find a way of making sound, using breath or wind
Devise a signalling system for communication that can be read from afar
Move apart until you reach the edge of the audibility of your partner's sound
Be playful along the edge of audibility

Create a score using marks on paper, or found materials upon the ground

For the river mouth and beach:

Gather
Create a disturbance, return to calm

Tuning the river, or a flow of water

Low tide: Using rocks and found materials, find ways of altering, or tuning the
sound of the river flow
High tide: Using stones and found materials, find ways of harnessing tuned sound
at the point where the river enters the sea

Sit, reflect and capture through written or drawn response

*[From 'walking as practice' field trip with Conall Gleeson, Music and Visual Art (BA Hons), Faculty of
Arts, University of Brighton. With thanks to Rosie Smith for inviting us to take off our shoes.]*

39. Perhaps we are like stones

The landscape of Swaledale, North Yorkshire, seems mainly stone. The lower hillsides are patterned by dry stone walls, which box and demarcate the landscape. Higher up, the green lushness of the enclosed fields gives way to the wide skies of the moors. There are still walls here, which snake off into the distance and over the crest of the hill, dividing one expanse of brown-purple heather from another expanse of brown-purple heather. Sometimes it seems as if the walls are not to keep anything in, or anything out, but rather to gather some of the infinity of stones. To harvest the stones that are the produce of the soil, pushed up by frost, exposed through erosion and time.

These are stones that have been worked, handled, selected; these are stones that seem to speak of history and pre-history and people and place; stones that talk.

About half way up Swaledale, grid reference 982972, there is a path that is more like a stonefall. It rises steeply from Low Lane to High Lane, cutting across contour lines and taking the walker from the dark enclosure of the dale bottom to the openness of the moor. Its steepness, its stoniness, its passage from darkness to light, gives the walk and the walker (for the two become one) a giddy sensation. It is a kind of transportation.

I have made this walk four times. On two occasions I have risen early and made the walk alone, in the cold and semi-darkness of predawn. On two occasions I have returned a little after sunrise with a group of MA students, studying variously theatre, fine arts and music, who I have brought to the Dales to remove them from their different but respectively familiar studios and comforts of practice and thought.

As we begin the ascent together I give instructions: to walk in silence and apart; and to repeat to ourselves a mantra, taken from Susan Griffin's book *A Chorus of Stones:* "Perhaps we are like stones; our own history and the history of the world embedded in us".

With these words in mind we walk. Together and alone we transport ourselves form Low Lane to High Lane. At the top we stop, panting, collecting our breath and our thoughts. As the saying goes, these stones can talk. Together and alone we stand there and listen. And wonder what they are saying.

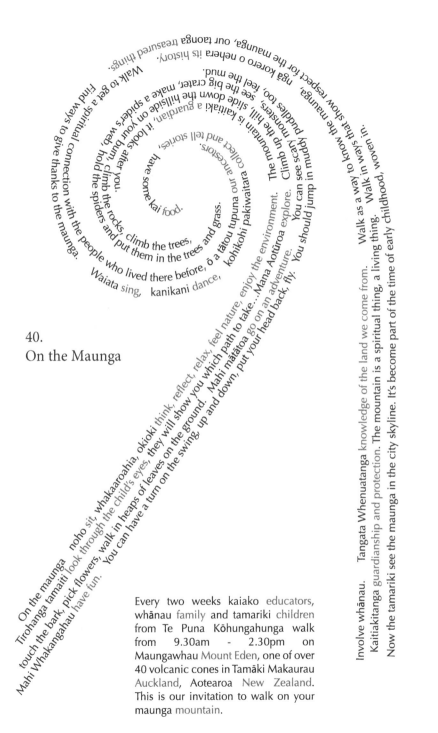

40.
On the Maunga

On the maunga noho sit, whakaaroahia, okioki think, reflect, relax, feel nature, enjoy the environment. Tirohanga tamaiti look through the child's eyes, they will show you which path to take...Mana Aotūroa go on an adventure. You can see scary monsters too, feel the mud. Mahi Whakangahau have fun. You can have a turn on the swing, up and down, put your head back, fly. You should jump in muddy puddles. Mahi matatoa go on an adventure. touch the bark, pick flowers, walk in heaps of leaves on the ground. Climb the big crater, make a spider's web, hold the spiders and put them in the trees and grass. climb the rocks, climb the trees, Waiata sing, kanikani dance, kohikohi pakiwaitara collect and tell stories. ō a tātou tupuna our ancestors have some kai food. The mountain is kaitiaki a guardian, it looks after you. slide down the hillside on your bum, see the big crater, feel the mud. ngā kōrero o nehera its history. Walk to get a spiritual connection with the people who lived there before, find ways to give thanks to the maunga.

Walk to know the maunga, our taonga treasured things. Walk in ways that show respect for the maunga, ngā kōrero o nehera its history. Walk as a way to know the maunga. Walk in.

Involve whānau. Tangata Whenuatanga knowledge of the land we come from.
Kaitiakitanga guardianship and protection. The mountain is a spiritual thing, a living thing.
Now the tamariki see the maunga in the city skyline. It's become part of the time of early childhood, woven in.

Every two weeks kaiako educators, whānau family and tamariki children from Te Puna Kōhungahunga walk from 9.30am - 2.30pm on Maungawhau Mount Eden, one of over 40 volcanic cones in Tamāki Makaurau Auckland, Aotearoa New Zealand. This is our invitation to walk on your maunga mountain.

41. In One Step

Walk for a while. At a certain point you stop. *This is your selected starting point.* Look around in all directions. Explore with your eyes and your ears where you are. Take your time. Say: "I have never been here before". You are going to take one step. Forward. Look ahead. How far can you go in one step? While you empty your left leg, move your weight slowly over to your right leg. Investigate the structure of the soil. When all your weight is placed to the right of your body, carefully lift your left foot. Feel the heel off the ground, bringing the entire foot into the air. You float, you levitate, above the ground. You struggle with balance and gravity. Rest assured that the ground will be there for you. You see far out over the landscape. Accept what has been and what is to come. Take a deep breath. It is time for a decision, where will you put down your foot? Chose a spot carefully. Heel against the ground. A fall down forward. The left foot is on the earth again. Weight transferred. Look ahead, but perceive with your back what is behind you. Say: "I'm here". Listen to the resonance.

Turn around to see if you have left any footprint.

42. Intertidal Walking

Three hours before low tide…

Descend the cliff

Scramble along the boulders

        (LOW TIDE)

        Slack water & wait…

                Scramble along the boulders

                  Ascend the cliff

                Three hours before high tide.

Watch people and movement passing by.

Observe the rhythm, the pauses, what is moving and what is not. Notice random and obvious relationships between different things.

The space is performing for you.
Witness two or more performances, decide when they end, then give them a title.

Walk in between two things...

...two people, two objects, one object and one person, a crack on the floor and a flying bird, a signpost and a shadow, writing on a wall and a passing car....

The two things can be close to each other or really far apart.

The landscape becomes a constellation of constantly changing landmarks that you can move through, and your threading path creates a connecting web and map between them.

Walk on your own, follow moving things...
...people, shadows, birds, water...

Follow their path with your footsteps.
Follow with your attention, with your eyes and with the whole body, follow with your nose, your back, your right shoulder...

What is the shape of their path? Consider your distance.

Stay with one path for a while, then switch to another.
Let yourself be taken on a journey.

Re-orientate the whole body to observe and reframe what you see.

Stay and let things move through your visual frame.

Notice:
Your body in connection with the ground.
The space below your feet and above your head.
The edges of your visual frame.

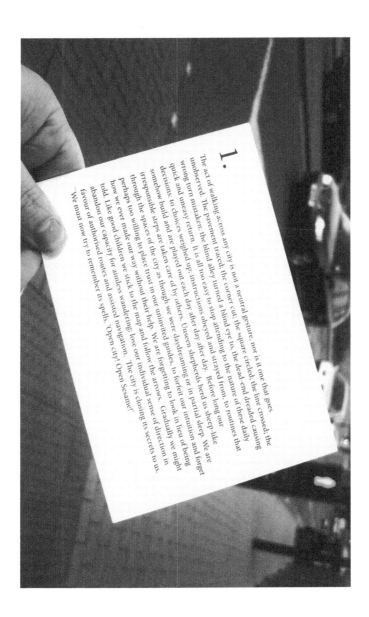

1.

The act of walking across any city is not a neutral gesture, nor is it one that goes unobserved. The pavement traced, the corner cut, the square circled, the line crossed; the blind alley turned a blind eye to, the dead-end dreaded causing wrong turn mistaken. It is all too easy to stop attending to the nature of these daily instructions obeyed day after day after day. Before long our quick and uneasy return. Unseen shepherds herd us sheep-like decisions: to choices weighed up; or by others, to forfeit our intuition and forget somehow build and are played out each day as though we were daydreaming or in partial sleep. We are irresponsible steps are taken care of by others, to look in lieu of being through the city as though we were daydreaming or in partial sleep. We are perhaps too willing to place trust in our uninvited guides. Gradually we might how we ever made our way without their help. We are forgetting to look in lieu of being told. Like good children we stick to the map and follow the arrows. The city is closing its secrets to us. abandon our capacity for aimless wandering; lose our individual sense of direction in favour of authorised routes and assisted navigation. 'Open city? Open Sesame!'

We must now try to remember its spells.

From: Clare Qualmann (c.qualmann)
Sent: 24 May 2014 13:29
To: Claire Hind (C.Hind)
Subject: Re: Ways to Wander project

Hi Claire,

I'm really enjoying the threads that this discussion (and the project of compiling these 'ways') throws up, especially the fruitfulness of the 'call and response' (and, yes, it would be a great way to compile vol. 2). They remind me of some formative moments in my experience of artworks, and how these have shaped me as an artist.

Your points about maps and scores remind me of when, as an A-level art student, I first came across a book of John Cage's scores. I was first attracted to them visually, as drawings, and then remember getting very excited about them musically. I suppose they were enthralling because before then I didn't realise that these worlds could collide: music, drawing, conceptual art, scores. They opened up a whole way about thinking about art and experience - that artworks can actually do things - not just be. That links to where I am now with making work — especially walking work — thinking about the experience of the person walking as the artwork, constructing elements of that experience and then releasing it — allowing it just to happen, and to be what that person makes of it. Those John Cage scores led me to Fluxus, and to other artists using instructions, rules, games and scores. Using rules to make visual works was liberating — just follow the rules, no need to worry about what it's going to look like, no need to decide what you want it to be, just do as you are told and it will come into being.

It brings to mind Peter Liversidge's proposal in *The Art of Walking: a Field Guide.* "I propose that you put down this book and go outside". That this comes on the 4th page of the book, before the introduction, makes me smile. I like the idea that actually I shouldn't read this book, I should put it aside and go for a walk instead. It reassures me that the fact that my bookshelf at home is full of walking books unread beyond the first few pages is fine.

My point is that I take great pleasure in following an instruction; I relish the combination of structure and freedom that rule-based works give me.

Clare

45. The city as a site of performative possibilities

Group

The Gaze of the Still
What are they looking at? Start at a statue and follow its gaze across the city. Stop when you encounter another statue and walk in the direction it is looking. What are the unspoken conversations between memorials, mannequins and figurines in the city?

Hugging Feet
Physically circle the parts of the city you love, holding it in a walking embrace. End with a circumnavigation of the city itself.

Pairs

Shadow & Light
Decide on a destination and walk there. One of you must stick to the shadows, the other must avoid them.

space & SPACE
Decide on a destination and walk there. One imagines they are claustrophobic, the other agoraphobic.

Alone

Sshhhh
Find the quietest part of the city without going indoors.

Wind Feet
Follow the wind and sail with your feet like artist Tim Knowles. Where will you land?

46. Wolf Trot

Movement instruction

- Lean forward, let yourself be pulled by the sternum until you fall into forward movement (walking). Do this in a big anti-clockwise circle.
- Let the arms hang to the sides, then increase momentum until you come to a 'trot' where the arms and everything else rotates around your centre line (looks a little funny). The movement is faster than walking, a little slower than running. Make sure your movement, while being loose and relaxed, maintains a certain body tone - easily controllable through the sound of your movement on the floor.
- Keep looking peripherally and keep your thoughts in the here and now.
- At the end of each session change the direction of the circle, making it faster and smaller until you find an end. Try out taking hands at the end and finding a step-rhythm together if you are in a group.
- Keep wolf trotting for 30-60 minutes.

Scores to play with

A) Keep the wolf trot going for at least 30 minutes and slowly 'scan' your body - skeleton, muscle, other systems. Don't lose the peripheral vision and here and now at any time!

B) Find one or more trotting buddies for a wolf trot outdoors in one big circle (i.e. in a park) anti-clockwise, then in a small circle clockwise.

C) Do not decide on a circle beforehand with your buddies, but let your bodies decide jointly; trot on the spot at crossroads until there is a shared physical, non-verbal decision.

D) Find ways to focus your attention: inwardly, outwardly (such as auditory perception, attention to colours, etc...)

E) Make a Wolf Trot-map of your home town: start where you ended last time, exploring your town anew with a specific awareness.

Trotting can be seen as a moving meditation and thus as a spiritual practice, but can also be used as a preparation for creative work. Depending on the situation - alone, with a partner, in a group, in/outdoors, specific intention - the experience will vary a lot.

47. Love at First (Site)

There are moments whilst being with others when our position in the everyday order of things is interrupted in ways that cause us to stop and reconsider social space as we understand it.

These interruptions might be things we overhear, something or someone that catches our eye, or a thought that enters our head from nowhere without warning.

As moments these phenomena cut through the routes of our lived experience, punctuating our trajectories and disrupting our paths. They are what geographer Doreen Massey might describe as events of place, and if we chose to think a little harder about their relevance and possibility, we might stand the chance of unlocking the creative potential of these events.

What happens if these infra-ordinary disruptions to our walks are treated as sites of love? Does the potential beauty of our negotiation of the city reveal itself, even if only for the split second it takes to make eye-contact?

Here the artist's inbox becomes a second site for the collection of texts that evolve from the agreement to fall in love with those we encounter during a walk in the city.

Love at First (Site) – some directions

As a participant in this performance of falling in love, you are asked to walk out into the city streets, but during this walk you are invited to sharpen your lens on the moments and connections that would normally pass without being noted.

Look around as others walk among you, and imagine how you might fall in love during these moments in time and place.

Who and what makes you conscious of your walk, and what happens if you agree that just for a moment you are able to fall in love?

What are the fictional narratives that take place as you wander whilst falling in and out of love?

As you wander through the city in this way, a shared space is produced where the city's innumerate fictional love stories overlap: First Site.

You are invited to take note of these moments as they occur and, once they are noted, to email them to citywandering@gmail.com

This account is a place where these encounters accumulate; a Site of fictional love made possible through wandering.

48.

Materials: Tennis ball

Setting: Urban

Method: Take a tennis ball and, as you walk, proceed to bounce it against the various surfaces that cross your path. Special consideration should be made to try to bounce the ball continuously, allowing it to transition from surface to surface, dictating your pace and direction somewhat. Continue your walk focusing on the sound of the ball bouncing, and the surfaces it interacts with.

49. Waylaid Walking (inspired by Walter Benjamin's practice)

"Quotations in my works are like robbers by the roadside who make an armed attack and relieve an idler of his convictions."
(Walter Benjamin from *One Way Street*)

As you walk along alight on the poor objects that illuminate the use and embodied history of a place; arrested by the thoughts conjured out of that object, material or surface, record that idea or your thought-feeling as a fragment of words.

Later, when you have finished walking, thread together these quotes as a string of words and fragmentary thoughts.

You can do this on your own or as a collective activity with two or more companion walkers, mixing together the waylaid materials.

50.

Psithurism n. the sound of wind whispering through the trees

9° C. Humidity 20%. Wind S.

Walk by the canal until you reach the church then take the next right under the wooden beam.

Pass the workmen placing bags of gravel and catch your reflection in the silver panels on your right. Fold it carefully.

Follow the path to the left and over the bridge; two men sit arm in arm beside their stall.

Don't be drawn in by waiters outside restaurants. Look up and see the graffiti arrow; follow it.

Walk through the square with the big stone well and turn at the glass animals. You hear a dog bark and chairs clatter.

A church bell chimes and you smell red wine. When you reach the bridge wait for me there.

I stood with the constant motion of moving bodies, the never ending rocking of the water. A boat skimmed through the moonshine scattering light into the sky and then was cut off by the curved eye of a bridge. There. There. Bells were sounding and people began to disappear around sharp angles of street corners and over steep walkways.

8° C. Humidity 20%. Wind W.

Turn left. The cobbles on the pavement will become smaller and you will pass under a neon sign.

Past the formaggiaio and through the narrow street. You will see a green painted door.

Look up and there is an old lady watching out of a square window. She is dressed in a dusty shade of pink like the inside of a clam and her long grey hair hangs loosely down her back. Stay for a while.

7° C. Humidity 10%. Wind E.

When you reach the market you will see a dog tied to a post; turn right and over the bridge. You are nearly there. People gather outside drinking spritz and you pass the school. Wait by the wooden door.

51. A Certain History

At sunrise, commence walking clockwise around the periphery of your town or neighbourhood. Count your footsteps, left and right separately, for the first five minutes then any time you wish afterwards.

Stop and draw a tree on your right. If you meet anyone on the walk observe their height and gender and whether they say hello to you and what type of hello— cheerful, brusque or mumbled.

Then do the same for what is closest to your right foot. When you stop for your morning break, what on the ground is closest to your left foot?

Notice how many houses you pass, whether they are one or two storey high, how many windows face you and whether there are any lights on.

How many objects are there? Please describe and list them in your notebook by size, colour, and texture.

Mark down the information in your notebook beside the current time.

Observe the texture of the walking surface— At the fifteen minute mark, estimate the number of cracks, stains, stones, etc in an area of your choice.

draw the tree nearest you in as much detail as possible.

Continue your walk when you are finished drawing.

Turn around 360°

Is there anything of the same colour in the area?

Measure the first stop sign you meet for height and width.

How many individual gardens do you see on your left, how many shrubs, are there any garden ornaments?

of your environment. the details observing Continue walking

Document the information in your notebook.

Stop and count the clouds, the trees, the insects and the birds you see right now and write the information in your notebook.

52.

Nostalgic and Pre-Nostalgic Drifts
(for those who know the City well)

Revisit scenes from your past and see how they're getting along without you. Look into the back gardens of houses you used to inhabit. Commemorate in chalk special places on the pavement where you said 'Goodbye' or had a memorable conversation, or kissed. Lay a wreath on the site of a memory you want to put to rest.*

~

Leave small architectural models around, for people to re-plan your city with.**

* Previously published in *An Exeter Mis-Guide* (Wrights & Sites, 2003). Reproduced with permission.

** To be published in *The Architect-Walker* (Triarchy Press/Wrights & Sites, 2015, in press). Reproduced with permission.

53. "Welcome to..."

"Welcome to..." is a form of guided walk led by someone who knows little or nothing about the location in which the walk takes place. "Welcome to..." invites the local population to construct a guided-walk of their own town or area. Bragging, confessions, digressions, ear-bendings, facts & figures, hidden histories, information, opinions, picaresque peregrinations, rants, raves & reminiscences, shaggy-dog stories, tall-tales and urban myths combine to present an alternative narrative to the 'official' guided walk or tour.

In terms of producing this walk, you should spend one day in the locale (a place you know little or nothing about) conducting ad-hoc interviews and creating a route from this material. Chat with anyone and everyone, tell them what you're doing and engage them in conversation. Record this, if they are happy for you to do so. Present the walk the following day – this creates a sort of echo of the dialogic and sociable practice of the previous day's discussions, interviews and material gathering; revealing and reveling in a particular sort of mobile palimpsestic practice.

Although the walk takes a specific route, the content may or may not refer directly to the landscape in an overtly geographical sense. When asked to talk about 'place', people often talk about *themselves in place* and, as such, the local terrain acts as an aide-memoire to personal accounts of place as lived space.

54. Ways to reflect

What is the conscious experience of the wander, what is remembered?

How much of what is remembered is reduced to significant moments?

Interpret those significant moments through specific lenses such as: *Autobiography. Human Geography. Play Theory. Feminist Geography. Public Memory. Intercultural Geography. Cultural Memory. Biography. Psychogeography. Choreography. Ethnography. Phenomenology. Ecology. Human Rights. Environmental science. Aesthetics. Other.*

- - -

Select a photograph/image from one of your 'wanders'. Research the place where you took the image through one, or a variety of the following:

Geological history
Political history
Cultural heritage
Local history
Contemporary history

Create a collage of written statements from your research findings onto/over/below the photograph.

- - -

Mark out on a page 12 squares using a pencil. Create a visual response in each square from 12 memories experienced on the 'wander'. The rules are as follows for each square:

Starting anywhere inside the square
Draw only 3 lines to a square
Lines do not have to be straight
They can curve, meander, and circle
When you lift the pencil off paper that is the end of one line
You need to stop when the pencil touches the side of the square
Repeat for each of the 12 squares.

authors

1. River Rural; River Urban: Roger Bygott

A visual artist looking for charge in the body, energy in the land, play in process, and delight in expression.
roger.bygott@gmail.com ¦ www.rogerbygott.com

2. Feeling and Touching: Debbie Kent

Debbie Kent is a London-based writer/performer; she makes work reimagining the city as half of collaboration The Demolition Project.
dejakay@gmail.com ¦ thedemolitionproject.com

3. Ranulph Glanville

The late Professor Ranulph Glanville was a cybernetician, design researcher, theorist and multi-platform artist/designer/performer.

4. Crossing Paths/Different Worlds: Romany Reagan

A PhD candidate at Royal Holloway, Romany's practice explores heterotopias, liminality, human geography and performing heritage in Abney Park Cemetery.
Romany.Reagan.2012@live.rhul.ac.uk ¦ https://abneyrambles.wordpress.com

5. Teleconnection Teledirection: Townley and Bradby

Townley and Bradby are a collaborative practice. They make work in spaces that are already being used by someone else.
townleybradby@gmail.com ¦ axisweb.org/p/townleyandbradby

6. I Cannot See the Summit from Here: Alison Lloyd

Alison's practice involves walking alone, for considerable distances, keeping off the paths where possible, striding out through moorland and mountainous areas.
alisonlloyd01@gmail.com ¦ www.alisonlloyd.co.uk

Interruption: Carl Lavery

Professor of Theatre and Performance at the University of Glasgow, Carl has written widely on contemporary performance.
carl.lavery@glasgow.ac.uk

7. Off-the-Grid Walking cARTography: Bronwyn Preece & Similkameen O'Rourke

A multi-disciplinary improvisational eARThist and pioneer of earthBODYment, Bronwyn lives off-the-grid on a remote island off western Canada. Similkameen is homeschooled, an avid rock-climber, aerial silks artists and horse rider.
improvise@bronwynpreece.com ¦ www.bronwynpreece.com

8. Going in Circles: Alexander 'Twig' Champion

Walker, Sculptor, Poet
ajlchampion@gmail.com ¦ alexanderchampion.co.uk

9. Walk with Me: Helen Frosi (SoundFjord)

Preoccupied by collaborative and cross-disciplinary practices, Helen Frosi is motivated by the creative, social, and political dimension of sound.
helenfrosi@mac.com ¦ www.soundfjord.org

10. The Underpass: Simon Pope

London Walking marked the start of a decade-long preoccupation with walking as contemporary art, and its various modes of sociality.
si.pope@gmail.com ¦ tinyurl.com/simonpope

11. Maternity Leaves: Lizzie Philps

Artist and performance maker, lecturer, PhD candidate. Exploring the performed maternal through the lens of walking practice and its documentation.
fullbeamlizzie@gmail.com ¦ www.fullbeam.org.uk

12. Perambulator: Clare Qualmann

Clare Qualmann is a London-based artist who uses walking to engage with people and places.
cqualmann@hotmail.com ¦ clarequalmann.co.uk

13. Walking in Drains: David Prescott-Steed

David is a writer, sound artist and urban explorer. He teaches art history at the Academy of Design, Australia.
dprescottsteed@gmail.com

14. Notes to the Novice Pedestrian: Robin Smith

Robin teaches sociology at Cardiff University. He studies and writes about public space, mobilities, interaction and homelessness.
smithrj3@cardiff.ac.uk ¦ www.cardiff.ac.uk/people/view/38088-smith-robin

15. Andrew Brown

Andrew facilitates experiences designed to expose that which is typically overlooked, including signifiers of the irresistible processes of change.
andrew@taktaktak.co.uk ¦ artwalking.org

16. Following forgotten Footprints: Bridget Sheridan

A walking artist teaching art in Toulouse University, Bridget's art questions the relationship between walking and memory, using photography and writing.
bridgetsheridan@hotmail.fr

17. Way from Home: Misha Myers

Misha creates and writes about located, participatory and digital performance work including games, sound walks, digital artworks and live performance.
dr.mishamyers@gmail.com ¦ www.wayfromhome.org

18. Step-by-Step: Neil Callaghan and Simone Kenyon

Callaghan & Kenyon work in collaboration to create choreographic and movement based works for the studio, social, urban and rural environments.
neilandsimone@yahoo.co.uk ¦ www.neilandsimone.co.uk

19. City Centre: Tom Hall

Tom Hall lectures in urban ethnography, sociology and anthropology at the Cardiff School of Social Sciences.
hallta@cardiff.ac.uk ¦ cardiff.ac.uk/people/view/38161-hall-thomas

20. Play the City: Helen Stratford and Idit Elia Nathan

They collaborate on projects exploring people's interaction with complex ideas within challenging and familiar spaces in performative and playful ways.
hi@playthecitynowornever.com ¦ www.playthecitynowornever.com

21. Walking with my Dog: Annie Lloyd

Annie is co-director of Compass Live Art, curates the Compass Festival, Leeds and is a member of Live Art UK.
alloyd50@gmail.com ¦ compassliveart.org.uk

22. Phil Smith

Phil Smith is a writer, ambulatory researcher and performer, member of Wrights & Sites, and author of *On Walking*.
mythogeography@gmail.com ¦ http://www.triarchypress.net/smithereens.html

23. Long Shore Drift: Jess Allen

Jess is a stereotypical dreadlocked-flexitarian-ecofeminist (sometimes aerial) dancer, walking artist and academic with a yurt, horse and dog.
hedgesprite@googlemail.com ¦ allinadayswalk.org.uk

24. Walker: Barbara Lounder

Barbara Lounder is an artist living in Nova Scotia. She teaches at the Nova Scotia College of Art and Design.
blounder@nscad.ca ¦ barbaralounder.ca

25. The Closer Walk: Marie-Anne Lerjen

Specialist in culture management, museology, languages, walking and singing Marie-Anne's art practice includes installations, performances & publications.
info@lerjentours.ch ¦ www.lerjentours.ch

26. Walking Ideas: Vinko Nino Jaeger

Graduated with honors from the Academy of Fine Arts Vienna. Studied Contextual Painting and Department Object Sculpture.
www.vnjaeger.com

27. Folding Paper Listening Trumpet: Karen McCoy

McCoy, artist, teacher in sculpture at Kansas City Art Institute, Missouri, has worked across the USA, in Europe and Asia.
kmccoy@kcai.edu ¦ karen-mccoy.com

28. Blake Morris

Blake is a postgraduate researcher at the University of East London focused on group walks as an artistic medium.
walk@thisisnotaslog.com ¦ http://thisisnotaslog.com/

29. The Best of all possible Places: Nick Tobier

Nick is an artist born and raised in New York, now wandering in Detroit.
nick@everydayplaces.com ¦ everydayplaces.com

30. The A-Game: Thomas Bolton

Tom Bolton is a writer and photographer, author of Vanished City and London's Lost Rivers: A Walker's Guide.
teabolton@hotmail.com ¦ teabolton.tumblr.com

31. A walk for Seaton Carew Beach: Chance Marshall

Chance Marshall is a walking artist who has an interest in the mutual construction shared by identity and place.
chance-marshall@live.com

32. How to Wander Lonely as a Cloud: Penny Newell

Penny Newell is a poet based in the English Department at King's College London. Her PhD thesis is on clouds.
penny.newell@kcl.ac.uk ¦ pennynewell.wordpress.com

33. Chip Walk: walkwalkwalk

walkwalkwalk: an archaeology of the familiar and forgotten is a collaborative project by Gail Burton, Serena Korda and Clare Qualmann.
info@walkwalkwalk.org.uk ¦ walkwalkwalk.org.uk

34. Walking with Limited Longevity: Gary Winters and Claire Hind

Claire Hind collaborates with artist Gary Winters exploring writing and play through live performances, visual exhibitions and walking projects.
info@garyandclaire.com ¦ www.garyandclaire.com

35. Walking in a Gallery: Carl Lavery

(See 'Interruption' earlier.)

36. Transecting: Bram Arnold

Bram is an artist who started with walking and kept going, into ecology, performance, drawing, writing, installation, academia and education.
bramthomasarnold@gmail.com ¦ bramthomasarnold.com

37. Radically Walking: Chris Green

Chris Green is an artist and academic. He will begin a collaborative practice-as-research PhD in September 2015, at MMU.
chrisgreen4000@gmail.com ¦ greenandowens.wordpress.com

38. For the River Valley: Jane Fox

Artist and senior lecturer at the University of Brighton, Jane's arts practice embraces drawing, print, installation and collaboration.
jane.e.fox@hotmail.co.uk ¦ www.muttermatter.co.uk

39. Perhaps we are like stones: Matthew Reason

Matthew Reason is Professor of Theatre and Performance at York St John University (UK).
m.reason@yorksj.ac.uk

40. On the Maunga: Molly Mullen

Created by Te Puna Kōhungahunga, Māori medium early childhood education centre, with Molly Mullen, lecturer/drama practitioner, University of Auckland.
k.liley@auckland.ac.nz ¦ tepunakohungahunga.maori.nz

41. In One Step: Cecilia Lagerström and Helena Kågemark

Cecilia is a director, researcher and senior lecturer at the University of Gothenburg. Helena is an actress and tightrope walker. They form the Alchemists.
cecilia.lagerstrom@hsm.gu.se ¦ www.hsm.gu.se & www.alkemisterna.se

42.Intertidal Walking: Chris Mollon

Christopher Mollon makes durational performance, performance-installation, action art/art action and sculptural intervention. He lives and works in Bradford.
christopher.mollon@gmail.com ¦ www.christophermollon.com

43. Vanessa Grasse

Dance artist engaging in cross art-form collaboration, improvisation and site-specific performance. Walking is central in her movement research / choreographic practice.
vanessagrasse@yahoo.com ¦ www.vanessagrasse.wordpress.com

44. Emma Cocker

Emma Cocker is a writer-artist based in Sheffield and Reader in Fine Art at Nottingham Trent University.

45. The city as a site of performative possibilities: Kris Darby

Kris is an academic and artist exploring walking and the journey motif on the theatre stage and through sound installations.
darbyk@hope.ac.uk ¦ https://remapthemap.wordpress.com

46. Wolf Trot: Kerstin Kussmaul

Kerstin Kussmaul is movement researcher, artist and dance teacher, Myoreflex practitioner, IDOCDE founder.
info@gravityhappens.net ¦ gravityhappens.net ¦ idocde.net

47. Love at First (site): Steve Fossey

An artist and researcher based in Nottingham, UK, Steve Fossey's practice explores how social space is produced through performance.
citywandering@gmail.com ¦ www.stevefossey.com

48. Tobias Grice

Grice's work engages in utilising a tourist mindset in a familiar environment, exploring issues held in plain sight.
tobiasgrice@gmail.com ¦ tobiasgrice.tumblr.com

49. Waylaid Walking: Charlie Fox

Charlie is artistic director of counterproductions. They collaborate with artists and the public on projects that generate new artistic culture.
counterproductions.director@gmail.com ¦ counterproductions.me

50. Psithurism: Isabel Moseley

Isabel is an artist specialising in book art and printmaking and h**as** been involved in residencies in Venice and Switzerland.
isabelmoseley@hotmail.com ¦ www.isabelmoseley.co.uk

51. A Certain History: Linda Rae Dornan

Linda Rae Dornan is an interdisciplinary artist creating performance, installation and video art about language, place, the body, and memory.
lindaraedornan@gmail.com ¦ www.lindaraedornan.ca

52. Nostalgic and Pre-Nostalgic Drifts: Wrights & Sites

Wrights & Sites (Hodge/Persighetti/Smith/Turner) use disrupted walking strategies for playful debate, collaboration, intervention and spatial meaning-making.
wrights@mis-guide.com ¦ mis-guide.com

53. Welcome to…: Mark Hunter

Mark's research focuses on walking, memory and sociability, the politics of place and the notion of radical parochialism.
mark.hunter@icmp.co.uk

54. Ways to reflect: Claire Hind

Claire Hind is an Associate Professor at York St John University where she teaches a range of arts based practices
c.hind@yorksj.ac.uk ¦ www.garyandclaire.com

About the Publisher

Triarchy Press is an independent publisher of alternative thinking (altThink) about government, finance, organisations, society, movement, ambulation, performance, gressorial adaptation and the creative life.

Also published by Triarchy Press:

On Walking... and Stalking Sebald

Walking's New Movement

Attending to Movement

Nine Ways of Seeing a Body

Body and Performance

A Sardine Street Box of Tricks

Embodied Lives

Enchanted Things

For details of all these titles, visit:

www.triarchypress.net

Lightning Source UK Ltd.
Milton Keynes UK
UKOW07f1000270915

259325UK00012B/42/P